TIL

ROSALIND HUDIS

INDEPENDENT INNOVATIVE INTERNATIONAL

Published by Cinnamon Press
Meirion House,
Glan yr afon,
Tanygrisiau
Blaenau Ffestiniog,
Gwynedd, LL41 3SU
www.cinnamonpress.com

The right of Rosalind Hudis to be identified as author of this work has been asserted by her in accordance with the Copyright, Designs and Patent Act, 1988. Copyright © 2014 Rosalind Hudis
ISBN: 978-1-909077-44-7
British Library Cataloguing in Publication Data. A CIP record for this book can be obtained from the British Library.

Designed and typeset in Palatino by Cinnamon Press
Original cover design by Cottia Fortune-Wood. Printed in Poland
Cinnamon Press is represented in the UK by Inpress Ltd
www.inpressbooks.co.uk and in Wales by the Welsh Books Council
www.cllc.org.uk

Acknowledgments

In the development of this collection I am greatly indebted to the mentoring of my publisher, Jan Fortune, and also to the perceptive critiques and encouragement of poet Samantha Wynne-Rhydderch, and the poet and playwright, Dic Edwards. Also to my family for their constant support. Acknowledgements are also due to the editors of the following publications, in which some of the pieces, or earlier versions, have previously appeared, *The Journal, The Lampeter Review, Agenda, The Interpreter's House, Envoi, Jericho, The Book of Euclid (Cinnamon Press) Stand Magazine, Magma, Rack Press pamphlet 'Terra Ignota', Poetry London, (website) Poetry Review, (website) Ink Sweat and Tears, Poetry Salzburg Review, Aesthetica Magazine Creative Writing Anthology 2013.*

Contents

This collection is dedicated to my father,

Peter Hudis (1925 – 2008)

Tilt

Ascension

In this painting they are striving to float

although the gallery is a stillness
                heavy with beeswax,
where sunlight's meted out,
                    higher than you can arch
                              to see.

You follow each up-stretched neck,
the strain in brush-strokes, their tug to follow
                the Christ as he rises – whitened
his fingers vanish
beyond the frame.

There are mountains where yearly
                    the snow rim rises
higher than the last, its oxygen pulls forest roots
                    cells clued to a scale
of North, nosing for cool humus,
                for constellations
                  that frost-out the bear.

Yearly the calculations climb, numbers whiten
out of grasp, the bear's tracks
                lost beyond the frame.

Seasons May Resist Origami

We conjured their shape,
a symmetry
like folded napkins, above

the heads of all evidence.
We wanted to shake them out
for our children, as keepsakes:

the way you'd smell snow
before it fell, the length of cold
to unroll before spring.

Sometimes they'd play retro
turns for the twist of it: ice
roped our hair as we tied

the gulf
between blizzard
and door. My sister

in Boulder
flicks a text like a trick
of mind: they are watering

roses in December
in such heat. It blooms
like a new brand of loss.

North

travelled within us
– a bronze weight
in its crate of polar words.
We stored it in darkness, certain
we could crank open
the lid, slip into its folk-scape:
glass sky, charcoaled fir.

There were sensations troved
in the book of childhood.
How intimate it was, air
like cold river water
in our throats, sugar dawn
so brittle you could snap
a twig off it, eat. Snow tastes

like iron, leaves a pang
on the tongue, a fox wail.
My father was addicted
to north – each summer driving us
up primitive motorways
to its argued outposts. Pebble-dash
estates glazed to granite, Atlantic

Cheap Pianos

come and go
like marriages – the brief
heady ones balancing
a sediment of whisky
in a re-used tumbler
at the end, or the keys
stress-cracks have inched up,
like party nails eroding
weeks after the event.

We kept one
for its *fin-de-siecle* inlay,
its candle-holders mottled
with vintage wax,
an old queen, feathered
by echoes of gas-lit bawdy.
It played a boozed,
coquettish slide around
the sex of a harmony.

Another seemed too stern
for its small iron bones,
all black-stained mahogany
thick as scripture. We'd humped it
from a dank chapel, unprayed in
for years. It took five
good men to raise, but its rhetoric
was nearly gone - mothy
and thinned as an old heart.

I thought of the duty of voices,
suited, gathered in
from the last farms
beyond electricity, the echo
and cannon of them
in the chromatic sunlight,
how they might seep between
piano staves of wood
of wire, their pitch blurring.

Mynydd Bach

Up here
nothing but the scratch
of reeds
in wind and the bright
plate of sea. The Llyn

parts water from sky
like a soft knife;
a red kite arcs -
becomes the rhythm
of my boots on turf.

Even the peat is light
underfoot, healed
after ice and windmills
lift their girders as breath
disturbs the kestrel's feather,
or the small life of streams
continues

through the mist
from Chernobyl.

Trefoil, sphagnum,
meadowsweet
memoried with owl.

Beneath me, the earth
is map, its roots
spores, seeds,
small bones, stored

like codes. Today
in the farm downwind,
I saw Menna and Robert
driving their cows

to the top field.
Robert is slow,
his shirt loose.
Already the sickness
that took his neighbour
is taking him

Summer in Powys

We were driving over the border,
that tipping point of day when hills wash
into the skyline, and the last rinse
of low sun tells you there is still a handful
of time left to gather in the sight of cattle
steering towards a gate. It smelt like a festival,

smoke, hog-roast. When darkness
lapped across them, field after field
spat and flickered with bonfires.
Except this was the cull: all day
without break the work, the livestock
shot between their ears.

As their line grew, the chemical telegram
of fear would have shipped from beast to beast
while their farmer stood on, everything
out of his hands and his exits
taped off, spelled with disinfectant.
We passed a yard of sheep

rigid on their backs, black
legs in the air like mechanical twigs,
the vet slow motioned in a protective suit
like one sleep-walking through a film
where all the trees look burnt
and the sky is no longer a roof.

And to think like this
is to make anything permissible.
You told me how sheep trust
the call to be rounded up, won't
sense that this is other than the next
pasture ahead. But that's how we kill,

it makes no difference that it's summer,
the lenient time, chestnut trees
candled and over-arching, the rivers slow.
In line there is no season, only
the fall of hooves or feet
on tarmac, air pushing like a hand.

Italy in Gwalia

After Mario Ferlito, wall artist of the Baroque Chapel at the Italian
POW camp in Henllan.

A corrugated night made this,
rain's stutter on sleep-hut roofs.

Beef tins twisted
to columns,

sacks poulticed
to walls with water, flour,

stained lake-white, tidal
only as Ferlito's hand

moved, wrist aching.
His brush hailed those

who would rise towards him
through pigments of onion,

beetroot, grit
flecked coffee, smudge

of blackberries, trenches of fat or tar
on an improvised palette.

They came as Christ
and apostles, eyes grey, averted

but their skin fruited
out of garments, was warmth,

wheat fields of it, apricot of wives,
lovers, babies.

Palate

She scrapes mackerel out of the tin,
dresses it with olive paste, cloves
ewe's cheese, basil. She hungers
more than the last time. Her belly
is like an exile, strapped
to the life-raft of herself.

Later, in the bath it is marbled
with hyacinth, peony, a fugitive
dark red. It rises from fogged water
with a kind of authority, self-willed,
detached from the bed-rock of her hips.
The doctor has mined it

for meanings he preserves
in an Oil of Ellipsis.
He floats round the hard pebble
of one word, the little embryonic fist
of it. She's already guessed:
In her mouth 'Downs' tastes ferrous

with the clang of tongue
on palate, is declarative, weighted
as a lintel, as Deus, Decibel, Dictum.
It segues into the long
sea tunnel of own, of syllables
every pigment of her blood.

Guesswork

These hills are houseless, cropped for miles,
nothing but their own rain-ochred skin.

Trees, sometimes, at the skyline, locked
in an arthritic scowl to the wind.

Only walls split the pattern, scrawl,
up slopes, or flash routes from a distance,

where low sun unearths a strand of quartz
thin as a palm's lifeline. It might be

the seam of a space where the waller
paused to measure how one stone

could set or break his patient
two miles of boundary. Not weight

on his mind, but tilt
to carry the years, the chipping

of beetle or ice, matter's slow
fold in. His rhythm of guess

and risk folds out the land.

Ultrasound

In this cave-room we watch
until a baby hardens
out of the liquid wax
light pours on a black screen.
It must mould to dichotomy
it seems – the good one
flickering in and out
of a perfect equation,
or the bad one
who doesn't add up:
a chromosome too many,
a glitch in the smooth
running chain.

Clearly my pendulum is pulling
towards glitch – the sonographer
calls and calls again
for the same
echoes, interrogates my belly
as if it could roll open
and confess.
But what I want to confess to
is enchantment – how held I am,
hostage in my own womb,
watching the signs for child
leap like floodlit salmon,
their rebel arc.

Salvage

I dreamed I was in water beyond a vessel
where babies were being born. It was all
black gloss in motion, liquid molasses.
Lights pierced and spasmed white
or electric blue. There was the sense
of a port on standby, ship horns, signals
meant and broken, voices became a low
concussion, peaked and fell and always
if I tried to board, I was waved away.

And I understood that we were at a border
where there was no transmission and no
codes to permit us. I woke, breathed clear
the room we had arrived in, still bare
dawn emptying its sediment, becoming
yellow, alive with pigeon calls,
sky half way risen, pushing
its holy crust. My newborn child there
like something salvaged, a tiny figurine,

wheat skinned, which I knew to be a passing
jaundice and her sloped eyes the unpassing
grain of her life. For now, all hours were tidal
cooled, re-heated. A mid-wife brought us tulips.
refilled my cup It seemed enough
– to moor ourselves in ebb
in surge, not in the babel of birds, engines,
voices. I watched the sunlight prove
door, ceiling, window, name-tag, cradle, breath.

Post Caesarean

Blue hour.
Afloat on morphine.
My baby shifts
through her squalls
and rotations.

The bed is lapping,
my feet going under.

(lights on half-life,
forgery of dusk
that never reaches darkness)

But something
is hooking me back:
veers – fades
as I reach.

(the cycle of tests ticks on
muted, remote,
as if under skin.)

When a nurse looms
out of the ceiling, I say
where is she? The twin,
my other one?

(in the window, dawn
beats under
a riddle of trees.)

The nurse glides
through my eyes, through
the claw prick
of a needle
She says: it's illusion,
          it will pass on.

Disclosure

The consultant announces
in his considered opinion
our baby is *a Downs.*
For a moment I consider

where unconsidered
would take us.
(And what would *ups*
have meant?)
He is so sorry
to bear such tragic news.
I looked at her our freshly-
titled daughter

who is busily getting
a full supper
from my breast,
and wonder at how quickly
two words can
dissolve all sounds

but what rushes like ocean
breaking on granite
and the backlash
panicking through a gale.

Still she unfolds
her repertoire of instructions
for mealtimes
and more mealtimes,
as babies do,
and studies us, her eyes
flecked like a sea gull's egg.

A nurse names them
almond eyes, (treats,
candied
from the beach stall?)
By their slope
will you know a downs.

With one hand
I hold her

with the other
claw myself ashore

There I find
a charter
of precaution and exclusions
glued to the glass nest
where our daughter mouths
at our milky circlings.

Nowhere does it say
welcome
how familial
the neat arcs of her mouth,
or babble like light rain
with which she wakes me
among the heart scraping cries
of other babies.
I was lucky.

We weren't the era
when they proffered
surgery to straighten
the delinquent angles
of a downs
because to fit
we must have beauty
and anyway we can
do anything
these days,
so why not that?

Still, they hand me
a list:
the defects
of a *downs*:
epicanthal folds, slanted
palpebral features, a flattened
nasal bridge, an undefined
mid-facial region, a down-turned
lower lip.

It was like a geography
of some pacific island, it's primordial
haze fragile and studied
only from the air. I saw

epicanthal folds
dipping and surging
like the arch of a whale's back,
steam, trellised by dawn fire,
rising from palpebral features, how
they might glisten like mica,
a long bridge of white rock
that lanced through the quiet forests
of the mid-region, the plunge of their branches

                              towards the sun.

Photograph

This is my daughter asleep in the morning,
one hand between the silvery poles
of her cot, that remind me of birch trees.

She's going to theatre soon:
the surgeon will snap her ribs
to reach a heart which can't wake

itself properly inside its blue forest.
She mustn't eat. So when she stirs and calls
my arms down for the first feed, I turn

to the wall. She beats a fist,
the size of a large bee, into air.
Her feet swim faster as if racing

a blind snow flood,
and I am the snow. Later
it's I who can't reach

my child so far under,
her face a locked, white egg
In the thicket of tubes.

Pact

Grand mother and grand daughter
compare scars
the long rouge channel
from collar-bone to rib. On either side
the breasts lie, like lazy fields,
stitches are small runnels
into the marshes,
although the grandmother, being eighty,
has a landscape after rain,
the grand daughter, being nine,
only surface. She is proud
of this connection, like a furtive pact
scratched between girls
in bushes beyond a gate.
When told the scar will fade
as any impediment might fade,
she rolls her eyes. What do *they* know ?

She's been further. Imagine the journey,
screen-light, green flickers across skin
that could be lengths below water.
The surgeon steers his needle
while his eyes track
the magnified creature, her heart
beached, dried,
beyond reach of its own tide-washes.
Its armour of ribs clamped open,
its blood-rivers diverted
down nerveless tubes to a reservoir,
a sterile, moonless, lake
valleys away from the body.
Imagine the loneliness of cells
aching for a message.
Imagine the return,
what hungers the heart brought back.

Heart Patch

For him to sew a patch
across the tiny abyss
in your four month heart,

the surgeon
must have you chilled,
your breath postponed

in a pause
outside the beat
you were set to.

As you slip
below the heat-line,
an arctic incubus

wells up through
your skin. We run
at the speed of death

down corridors
rimed with day-break
while nurses course alongside

snow-geese migrating,
unstoppable, urgent
as they press you

between thermals of wool.
When the wind lifts you
out of my arms to theirs

I remember this is the day
of solar eclipse.
The moon will defer the sun,

muffle its pulse,
draw night's simulacrum
through the lunch-hour

of junior physicians
while they settle off-time wings
on the courtyard benches.

Their sandwich foil
that unmeshes the sun
into fractions of a rose window,

will smoke over,
like a moment known
to all the work-force of hearts

in partial eclipse.
Later I'll forget
even to remember this,

subtracted from the daylight,
in a waiting room
on the rim of your theatre,

I'll think of the surgeon's hands,
dough pale and trimmed,
between butcher's and tailor's.

Topography

More delicate than the historians' are the map-makers' colors.

Elizabeth Bishop – The Map

She can't read but likes to crackle her fingers
over the surface of a map she has opened
batted and flattened into position beside me.

She wants to draw along the contours
of a story that flows out from her key place:
New York, home of *Friends the Sitcom.*

She thumbs it dead centre of everything,
even though her chosen terrain
hovers between bog-wastes

and Llandovery. I read somewhere
that ancient cartographers planted Jerusalem
at the kernel of every chart, the steady state

in a swelling floret of land mass,
tiny, angle-conflicted and garrisoned
with roofs, like an ageing mother

who always got taken along and always
had something to say about the menu.
My role is path-finder not giver

of the habitual view. When I trace
a meek thread and call it ditch, she storms
at me, no, that's where Ross kissed Rachel;

she means: lead me, lead me *there*
into the heart of this pale green valley of paper
in safety, go where I go, without history

getting between the lines.
Bishop was right – it's how you colour it
and on this webbing of routes across earth

that's skin deep wherever you go
my daughter paints in the chiaroscuro
episodes of a self she will be.

Colour Field
after Rothko

At sixty, was he glad of the greenhouse,
its dirty panes, webs that hid him ?

The tomato smell like a reflex
to his hands, though nerves had thickened,

fossilised touch – one moment
charging another. He'd wanted that much

for paint – the breach of it beyond
edges, the way it glowed

behind sight. Or the dark plum odour
of another person, the just audible

tack of their pulse, intimate but boundless
as the self, or a road – say, Highway 287

that red dust route whose promise
is Texas dawning on a loose horizon.

If he dozed, misted, it was to expand
his vanishing point while traffic slurred

on a freeway and further, barking
frayed at the limits of his mind

where dogs and guns in another night
were driving his childhood out

of Dvinsk to the boats, to a sky
that seemed self creating

Paint Chart A-C

Axurite for the triptych virgin and apostles
    layered together – marzipan people
        on a planetary cake, while underfoot
            a martyr is sliced cleanly as a goat.

Bistre for roasted beech, the year culled, a sting of embers,
    parks singed by acid, humus, that gravy
        ladled by great aunts on all forms of dinner, their brown
            baize rooms, their brothers, blown up in trenches.

Cadmium for gas sheen in Van Gogh's puddles, the yellow halos
    rimming Paris cafes almost the colour of sin, pear-light,
        a s picnic – the convertible a shining butter,
            Nevada, phobia, haze of exclusion zones.

Apollo Party

You were fired away one morning
in moderate calm.

Press, champagne: I wore a metallic perm, a frock
ice-cream safe, my breasts wired up, cogs
in the logistics. You, a cartoon, Ken doll
all tubes and padding – the rocket
slick as a wedding cake and just
about to pop. For the shoot it was

soda skies, peroxide
weather, All American
sun tans. We manned our poses
like a frontier – collateral
against the final rip
of atmosphere.

Sound Notes

You will know by now the cave-suck groan, anemones
under saline pools: these from *Joe Davis*

who, to transmit the score of our conception
recorded a dancer's vagina pulsing

onto discs he'd launch to the planets. Later he planted
a map of the milky way on the teeming glitter

of a mouse's ear. Silence sounded out
can hurt: radiation plays a guitar

into hollow, tin pan non-sequiters.
Lies create shape

for the shapeless.
In films, the unbearable

unfinish of a thermal blast was arced between
two strings of the heart:

a falling wall
a waterfall.

The Astronaut's Wife

All day she's watched breakers
self-consume. Now

lights fly down one
by one on the headlands
and she remembers the cold
flap-past of geese
through a window in Maine.
This is the worst time –

radio on news hour
steam in the kitchen
her ladling stew, but still
the sea's lunge
and stars hook at her,
fishing for the impossible
statistic of his return.

*

The other wives have warned her –
said the moon switches husbands
to the mean side

as if to float over
its rutted calcium
is an emptying,
a calamity of silence.

All day she's watched breakers.

Paint Chart M-N

Malachite for turquoise margins, that strip
    between walled and wild, the squire and wife forever
        foregrounded, stiff with silks. Or green skirts
            on Egyptian slaves, line-danced across a tomb.

Navajo the hot shade of boom years, popcorn, hint of satsuma
    lounge light of Ontario suburbs, upwardly
        mobile towards Magnolia. Plastery, tribal
            as a souvenir. Stains vanish into it.

Ochre for the burnt up cadillac
    on a road tilting
        into the future's light bowl,
            verges liked smoking pepper.

Tilt

My friend has this story, the one
of her premature birth, the one
where they swear she weighs
little more than the soul

where they tilt her like an effigy
on a polystyrene board
in the incubator, tell her mother
go home, forget. That night

under shawls, under rain,
the mother thieves her home
over-feeds her glucose

warms her burn-close
to a paraffin heater, giddy
on love and fumes.
Is survival a choice to know

better? Tonight she phones
in pieces, because she's old
and her choices aren't there
on the ground

of her body: less
fire, less water, less recovery.
She's swaddled in manuals

on soul-care, but where is love?
Have I heard of that state
where your body locks down
everything shunted in

and out through tubes ?
Still your mind rotates
on like something thrown off
in space. Does it ache

for rescue or see
from such distance,
the home lit cities ?

I look at the night,
stars like shattered bulbs and one
constellation a drunk woman
pinned down by surgical beams.

The Atomist in Exile

That crash wakes him: heart bullying
his ears, but night flaps only
waste bags in the yard. Somewhere
a fox cry ghosts the slip-road
off his mind. Later, their diagnosis:
a syndrome – *exploding head*

heard only in the head. Benign
and untrackable and *what were you on?*
his wife says. Just the usual suspects,
and often now the sense of not
quite getting it, or a name crossing
the junction ahead, then slurred

through a riddle of headlamps.
He's guessed his obits, his precision
lauded, 'patience' – no glamorous stunts.
Knows he should calibrate himself
to himself, to the void, find himself
out, his flicker along

the decay path, or blend himself
into the weave of his own effort,
work out in thin sample light
of dawn, (his muscles packed so long
into the microscope's pin-hole
dwelling among atoms).

Jews do tight places, he'd joked –
those years he'd pitched a lamp
into the belly of a coal mine, needing
oppressive air to breath.
Einstein, he'd say, had wanted that,
a tight answer, a lit particle

like a pin to hang reason from.
But often now the ratios slip
his reach and so much easier to sit
dumb and lose on a wicker chair
by his North ocean, the dun
churn of it, there, in his wife's eyes.

Nash i

Winter afternoon, the gas fire hisses,
drugs us into flock-papered quiet.

Our post-austerity street lies
in permanent recovery, chestnut leaves

smudging the pavements. There might have been
a line breached, a row drifting away

in another room to sulk itself out – dad's tetchy;
if I lap closer, he might give,

show me a book of paintings – I want Paul Nash
– that picture where the harbour leaks

through a deserted house as if inside
has crossed a different line, or ones where fields

are milky as fog or mushrooms, except the trees
have gathered too closely, like watchers on a cliff.

Oil in Blue

Outside this room it's summer, but Dad paints
snow, over everything, and most of it blue.
I climb the scarp of his back, peering in.

He's left all the people out, though roofs lock
together like the wall-mind of victims.
The traffic light is a red nerve, the street dead

end, no stilled cars. You'd find it hard
to move down the bone-white streaks of path
among all that blueness. There are windows

lit; I beat Dad's neck and ask him
what the people are doing, the people he lit.
I don't yet understand each room

is a past tense, has lost its keys, its hot cells
guttering out, one after one.

Invocation

whatever it was – the slow shutting off
of your lighted capillaries,
or the currents one by one unplugged
between us, whatever stories
we route to this aftermath –
I couldn't disable a sense of you
alive in the mortuary, of you struggling
to know where you were, to understand
the blue brick walls, the absolute cold.

As I rinsed beans after your funeral,
chopped the splayed chicken
for the faithful supper, it wasn't grief I felt
but betrayal for being voyeur
to this struggle. I wanted to reassemble you,
not as you were, the *remembered best,*
but mind-haul *you-in-pain* across every yard
of pavement, invoke us washed by drizzle,
the petrol taste of fog,

hearing the drum pulse of a helicopter
somewhere at the city's edges,
name each street, feel the frontal lash
of wind on a north corner, bring
your ghost to stand, twist-locked,
at my shoulder in the kitchen and I could say
that you were here and this was death.

For several days I breathed on empty,
kept you close, spelled out your traces,
the constellated stains of tea across an atlas
opened for my daughters to show the yellow
of equators, until my heart settled,
found its level in the wideness filling
each page, the receding oceans, deserts.

Paint Chart U-W

Umber – less than umbra, than the taut negotiations
   of black, zone of moths and scrabbled earth,
      of dryness at the heart of things, of eyes
         sparking behind smoke.

Verdigris – unimaginable once – how that tone could be vernal
   verifiable, verdant. The ways it died as a sense. How little
      subtlety could still be afforded. How Botticelli spread
         layer on layer, as if time was the achievement of green.

White – titanium, lead, lime, zinc, carnation, cream,
   the sheet over a crime scene, a portal
      of negatives, of shades of not saying
         or its reversal, its vanishing eye.

Not Said

A child on the doorstep scanning the path for ants
                                      or bugs. She won't launch
into the wideness of not inside, her flight-path hijacked
by particle zaggings, by tiny unsettlements.
Or a child taken on walks that pull the hours across
wind-stripped hills. She won't step over
                          the sheep dung, not for the horizon
her father chivvies into view. She's stalled

by something so small so multiple. What is embedded
in those soft bullets, blackened and clustered
in the dips and runches of grass, their fume
                          of smoke in the mouth ?
They cover the earth, like crossing
                          a stony beach bare-foot, sand beyond
bearing distance.

That time they camped. A coarse field. Cow breath.
Awake at dawn she unclips the flap. She hears
                          her father weeping, the sound
                              flattened behind canvas.
By the river she sits down. If she lowers in her feet, they eddy
dis-bodied as gloves. She's never been told what the weeping
                          means. It's her toes she recalls
floating as if unstitched, and the fume of dung in ground mist
and the distance beyond bearing back.

Feghoot

My East is flinted sea,
a horizon that leaves the sky
with too much scope. We're there,
tiny on a mat of sand, the only one
on beaches that keep laying
the same hands down like a pun
with no punchline, only their curve
softening to a paste, sea-kale,
fog, and the tern white
of Shingle Street, straight
as Lego, shorn off as if it can't finish
its sentence in the wind
from Russia. Close up

we're bunched under towels while dad
frets out a fire from sticks pulpy
with brine. He's telling us
the shaggy dog tale again, the one
where the Captain of the Ship
calls his men about him
to tell them
over and over
how the captain calls them
about him to call them
into the loop of a storm
with no eye. Sometimes dad tells us
the other one, the one where fuel

is piped under this beach, under
records of war, burns on the sea,
won't go out. Nights
after that I sweat
out of the same dream, the one
where fire blends me down to bone
no matter how many times
I jump into water. To get me
back to sleep dad tells me
the shaggy dog tale, loop over
loop. Words soften to a paste.
He keeps circling with the same hand
as if through fog.

Translation in Avocado

i

At the sink I scrape fat from knives,
remembering how before she slid
through a crease in the story
my great aunt buried her best blades
under the chicken poked earth.

I keep for her a scrag of moon
cut loose from its gossipy orbit
of anecdote and silence. Cleansing
is not a word it's equipped for. Nor
night at a bare table.

What would it take to leave nothing
for the risen meal ? They hid pans
below the cabbage, candle-wax, plates,
tins of salt, flour, treacle
dried fish, a violin, a compass.

ii

My grandmother, the survivor, stands
at a sink in her Wembley kitchen
and what I mostly recall is how lost
she is in avocado – all her wallstoned to it, all without portraits.

Granddad grows a swatch of mild grass
he calls *lawn*, three foot square
installs a bell that intones a perfect fifth
elongates the sound as if their rooms
had pulled themselves through

sliding doors, multiplied.
Behind them, new carpets, fittings
float, geometric, in one dimension.
My grandmother composes the knives
from Marks, cushions them on Satin.

Life-stage

On solo afternoons I'd dig through soil
my mother over-fed each spring, swearing
she could turn 'rubble' into loam.
I put her Midas mind into the trowel, churned

clay pipes, teeth, blue and moony cuttings
of perennial Delft. Metal things surfaced
in the flotsam chat of adults: how sea once
heaved a mine up our beach. It had horns,

the hulk of a slug and Minotaur mixed up.
For nights it cricked through dreams.
Afterwards, I wasn't the child hunting flints,
their planetary cavities and mauves held up

like a local miracle. It was all greys now,
wartime wire in the seaweed, fears watery,
or specific as cancer. Aunts sifted the gloom
for nuggets of explanation, milk-teeth hormones,

anything to begin the long medicine
of getting over. These days I bury, or butter
across my traces, gild, smudge, re-render
the snapped and scuppered lifelines.

Rolling the Soul

...and there's the one about Perel, my Lemberg forebear,
who thought her mother's soul had rolled into the samovar,
heard her pursed, upbraiding, voice inflected in the stream
of tea from spout, hairpin straight, sourdough black.

Not quite a dybbuk, but irritant- the gleam of her one
gold tooth snarking within the silver. Maybe through the night of
the crossing to London, great great Perel, leaden with great Perel
in her womb, vomiting salt, found comfort in that thought:

her mother co-tossed, blaspheming among the trunks.
In the blitz their samovar was seized or smelted – and where
her grandma rolled then was a jinx great Perel disowned,
rolling herself into the name of *Pearl,* and minted curls,

her tongue new polished to somewhere between Brent
and Queen mum, her unstained tea spoons bright as *Lewis's.*

The Women of my Childhood

as I veer out of the fog
of play in a brick-deaf yard,
back through a kitchen door,
are always bending
away into another act.

Their hands vanish into bowls
that loom like chapels,
or raise a coal bucket,
or wring dry the space
words have walked out on.

It's always their backs
that meet me, the dissolving shape
of things just done, the reel of bones
under house-coats, phrase
chained to phrase, pulled

ahead as I reach to grip
a pocket, laundered and empty
of the side-tracks a man might keep:
a dice, a coin, or pen-knife,
the glint, the leap, the cut.

Peeling

I was waiting for gran to raise
each potato, nude and wet

to the light, her fingers
raw-puckered,

survivors. I'd catch
the thumb's intricate speed

as it forced the peeler,
like a diver unhooking the welded

corsets of a wreck.
And what hits now is the clang

shut of her talk. The make-do
and bury of her hands, dim

under water, or sunk
to the wrist in a swamp of flour

and egg, or, to impress me,
unbandaging skins in one

sleight of knife. Always
the back of her head then.

If she turned to mind me,
I don't remember it.

Angle

Three times a day we'd teeter
her cup up the stairs – the clot brown
cockney tea she swore by – thick enough
to hold a scaffold of spoons.

Over-spill sloped in the saucer. Half-way
on the landing where we dreamed
up from spare light a ghost,
then wetted sheets in fear of it,

was the place to re-tip. Through her door
a shift, a breath of North, at night
the moon's chalk hair
tangled in net curtains

she'd hung across decades.
Once she flew to Canada, came home
bristly with triumph
that where we held the earth round for sure

she'd seen flat.
It was one over us
whose voices tickled under her floor-boards
but spoke of worlds

outside hearing as she floated
in a room that seemed tethered to the sky.

Gags

There is no manual for *how to sink*
gracefully. You can piece-meal a way down,
improvise a rope from things
the doctor said (*your heart is strong*)
build a resistance movement
of one, from what has worked before,
or filch from another script,
and hope the gags
will graft onto your time-line,
like the battery
they stitched inside his chest.

There is no manual. Chair-locked,
he re-lived how McNish guessed
and garnished a small boat into one
that echoed the template of rend-proof
vessel topping a fermented sea,
a Turner derangement
of paint, gravity and time.
Shackleton feared an illusion,
mere scenery – the varnish of flour
and seal-blood, the frame
re-mastered from wooden crates.

Terra Ignota

After your funeral, father, I asked what, in the years,
saddened you to a man who couldn't leave his house

without going back to check the locks three times?
Or whose feet picked over the stair-treads,

at .am, sniffed into darkness for smoke, whose hands
felt for the kettle to unplug it yet again?

Was it a habit of secrecy turned inwards,
interrogating the plaster work, the carpets?

Or that instability of those born Jewish
on sliding land – that gene-locked fear

you nursed and battled and tried to sail from
in a mind stashed with tins for emergency ?

*

My father, in his final illness, adrift
across an armchair, barely able

to tack the crucial space from hearth
to toilet, would watch each night

In Shackleton's Footsteps, the foraging
of one obsessive man beyond the skyline

of himself. Metal and snow
blistered light lanced

across his face, like a fractured
mayday from *terra ignota.*

But he locked eyes to the plot,
mapped with it strategies to push

beyond stalled ice-anchors and feet
whose nerves were shot. He had so many

years found relief in logic- a way to get
through, a compass for the blizzard

that falls and keeps on falling.

*

Through his last year as a sailor, he sat for nights
in the cabin of his small yacht that never

left the marina, hurricane lit, scratching
in a logbook the minutes of heft

to make sail out of the river-mouth,
as if he could slide

over the skyline of his bones,
hear the North Sea

break its free verse, saline,
across his skin. Or was it to be ready

for the sea-lock
to part, the current pull him

into unboundaried
open sea?

Civil Service

This morning my grandfather's ghost
reads *Jewish News* in a railway bar
where I've gone for coffee and retreat.
I burn my hands on the cup.
He's all there, the forensic neatness, hair
a Bakelite side-part, tailored
to his great coat. All five foot,
mostly trouser. Shoes polished
in the way shoes were polished
twice, in an age of officials.
He is hiding out, clearly, on a bench
of my mind between trains and pigeons.
In a moment I will leave
for Great Eastern's screech and clamber
towards glazed fens.
The track will dispatch the landscape
like bulletins from an edge.
Graffiti, stacked wire, wasteland.

It is a repeating journey
to my father who is dying.
Last week my grandfather's ghost
was grimed
steam on the carriage window.
Today he's come clean, sends a whiff
of his era, like a tonic.
He won't be less than a pin
striped, gold watch, memory
of his dapper departure to an office
in the Dept of Works and Recreation.

He won't see
how his son who is dying
drifts, vagrant,
off the shined-up remake
of their history in a new world.
thin as the soupy light.
Graffiti, stacked wire, wasteland;

This is a country
for old shades, but my grandfather
won't acknowledge it.
He won't be
a clipboard on my survey
among derelicts. Once,

his signature corniced
acts of repair, like a security rail.

String Theory

In the drawers of my childhood there was always string,
spooled against the hiatus of a moment

when a lamp-pull snapped or weight bearing sticks
couldn't take the strain. String –

as much a heal-all as rosehip tonic and the sticky
charm of castor oil. Or in school gangs

loose on asphalt, winding out
the borders of early friendship, we'd stretch

string over fingers that smelt of chalk and urine,
pinching and pulling taut, looping,

under and across until the cat's cradle
hummed between us like a live-wired fence.

Who keeps it these days? Emptying the coats
of my grandfather, a fix-it man who finally

hitched onto a world tied to screens,
I find talismans of string among the screwed receipts,

durable cotton handkerchiefs and overlooked pills.
He'd say there's a remedy for everything and most of it

hangs by a string. Like the dot to dot
of prescribed evasions

to the end. And the way
a memory loops

a memory
round its tail.

Rupture

There are days she stares
at the kettle, but can't retrieve
its connection to water. Or days
when the dry bristles of her brush
remind her of a cactus that flowered
every ten years, if she cared for it,
but how that brush could sooth,
re-wake her face, is lost.

There are days the phone rings,
but she can't re-map the way
her hands could bridge a room
to open or close the tap of speech.
Sometimes, she's forty years
back in a war-time booth,
upright among the broken
knuckles of the street,

scrapping with her boyfriend,
the moment when
the glass sides shower out
and, all around her, tenements
flower into a once in a lifetime
spasm of absurd heat.
She watches bloodied women
pour out, still in their aprons.

One carries space where her baby
was swaddled in a shawl,
while the city settles
in ashes across her hair.

Bordered

We were in one of those hollows
in the weather chart where frost
crimped the verges, but left snow
wherever we were not.
We could see it across the hills,
shipping its tonnage of light
back to us like a promise.

For once it was everyone else
time-locked on a motor-way,
trucks stalled in an arctic smur,
night circling like a border guard,
heavily coated and fingering
the myth of wolves in his pocket.

We'd been there in other years
so near home, with nothing to look at
but crows staking out glacial fields,
headlamps left on like a question,
and us, out of conversation. It was
the way everything stills at an edge,
becomes dangerous although no one
can tell you who is untrusted.

And for a time you are not banded
or identified, or known by lights
melting to a destination. You are
inconsequential as stone-crop
a beam crosses, or the ribboning
shadows dropped by a storm rise
of the crows to flight.

Migrants

They homed in across the valley, cleared
a cottage, decades empty, shovelled
owl shit, sheep mess, leavings
of disused time. They painted a tonic

ascent, deep ocean to pale blue
in a roll from living room to attic,
dug a pond in their reclaimed meadow
for the day to hinge its changes.

When the geese came, trouble-
shooting in formation, their cries
a circus of saxophones tuning,
a gun was borrowed, birds

downed for ruffling the surface.
But sky sharpens and softens
between rain-strokes, can't be
rooted, is never the same

hope twice. Nothing really settles,
No two harvests. No word that isn't
migrating from another. Here
One morning two hundred households

had signed up for a boat, sailed to Ohio.

Open Field

This is the month our paths become a green butter
in which you sink, while your boots fill with the night's rain
and you come in bearing news of unripened sweet-corn,

how summer can't be trusted. Our daughter's on a plane
to Colorado, where the High Peak's burning
down into the epidermis of cities as it hasn't for years.

Does my belief run the engine? It seems compelled
as DNA – like the willow arches
you'd bent for the French beans, so they'd grow

to form. You tell me: to throw an arc
between known and other, repeat it
often, is to make a shape of home.

I will put on my coat, my hood of tunnel vision
where the plane will return, the fires
time out, I'll sweep leaves – the furnace bail

of them, seismic as I tread them into ruts
become wells, lean in, pull back, like a child
rocking on the hip of darkness.

Above me vapour deepens, braids into smoke.

Closure

in Nevern Churchyard

He says: *stand by the yew trees.*
He angles his phone
to displace the sky doubling itself
in miniature, until her shape
comes clear like something
that shouldn't be there
yet is. She leans into the bark

shadows, stretch marks,
intimate as a map.
It smells like back-tide,
brackish, and of that close
must-dryness of moss
holding too long.
There's a kind of will

in the way the tree extends
its quiet to contain her – sunlight
falls short of her shoes, catches
grave-stones half lost to grass,
the parish families,
the week-spans
of babies who didn't make it,

the children who did,
but later died of typhus or in war.
Is she, to him like the backs
of people mounting a plane
visible but already elsewhere?
One press will hold her,
absolute for being absent.

Llyn Brianne

The reservoir stalled us, a shield
of quiet
after catastrophe,
as if that blanketing sealed in
water's coal flatness, its playing
out of inertia, glassy
with secrecies,
reversed firs
laid over, sky polished as a lens
for probing intimate structure.

And maybe aftermath is all you get,
however deep into the hollows
of stomata you peer, however many layers
you call a journey: *Outer bark, inner
bark, cambium, heartwood,
pith*. The roots are anchored
to shadow, the branches opaque
as a stem word,
radical,
theme.

We walked there, hunted the affixes
drowned with one farm and a fist
of valleys, broken, gloved
in sheen – limned out from text
the lost ferns,
globe flowers
tuned to less light, their fruit
silt-brown, their leaves
keel ridged, *ovaries
stigmata, pistils*.

Elan Reservoir

Bog miles are a long spill of rust, flat cloud and the road
a single feature snaked through rain that's veiled us

all day. Until the lake, an alpine face-lift stretched
as cellophane – too level between hills. No piecemeal

moss and fraying of things
going under in their own time.

At the museum of drowned farms and fauna
litanies of loss are framed – Shelley's house where Harriet

crushed blueberries for gin. Cast off in London
she dropped under the Serpentine.

Rock and water age alike, soft dulling, the seep
of lichen or weed, its binding.

Such lost slow dying
is not recorded here.

Retrieved perhaps down the valley where a chapel
has drunk in its years

for the roof to sag, a yew to flake blood bark, for swallow
droppings to fur panes

for panes
to stitch glass to sky.

Erosion

A year since we last climbed this path
to where the field's sentence
falls, unfinished, to a speechless glaze.
Sea; a single boat hovers
like a pause-mark. Already edges
are closer, there's less of anything
that stands for firm. Cliffs fritter
into air as if addicted
to an ease of giving
themselves away.

Balanced here, ruins of Monachty'r Graig
behind us, we could be something
salt-air has brittled, so porous
time could funnel through.
And it seems effortless to be this,
almost generous. The farm
eating itself from the inside, half-gone,
not empty, but spacious, loosening out
through a breach in the roof
where sky leans in.

West

was where the mainland floated its babies:
downy, off-shore landlets. You could take boats
to play among them, sample that edginess
of their DNA, hovering, but loosed from the chewed
mothering home-bulk. In this configuration
you could stray into thinner air, the magnetism
of brinks, cliffs the terns plunged for you.
This was our atmosphere, always within
and not within, our skins.

The hermits knew that, barnacled to a god
composed of weather. Wisdom was earned
by the hundred ways skin soaks,
smarts in gales or nourishes itself on light.
Rock stayed them, carved out a tension
the mind could surge from. Sea faced,
they patched bridges, mended the ferries,
were keepers of the lighthouse – gate men,
nursing life through elements.

Language Death

The Speech won't crumble fast; its vowels will break bread
                   between gums the way tectonic plates
          will go on speaking and shifting
                         the world's long gossip.

It will burrow for millennia if it has to,
                   in grit-stone, slag, a hare's pellet
          below smoking heather,
                         take the shape of what's to hand -

let the transitions of ridge to sky
          become syntax, water mutate
                   its wind-scurried particles, elide
                         into the river's throat. It washes

old teeth ripped
          from the hill face, dung
                   and gold-spined pebbles
                         to fit a word.

Skomer

i

Distance gave us rock.
But what I remember
is the strata of bird cries
how cliffs poured from them
like a hungry psalm.

There is nothing rooted
here that does not shape
to the life underfoot
a subsoil of wings,
of eggs sunk like ashes.

Catacomb of bird hearts
each an intention
each powered by exodus,
where salt is a marker
staining the wind.

ii

No parallel tracks run, just this
milk-stream skelter
through thrift and heather and barely
your shadow's waver to the brink.

You could turn back here,
or make a pact
with the day's spread cream.
Fulmars beat a warm fixative

holding the sea at ease.
There's nowhere metaphor
won't go and in time
will. For now it keeps

the poise of this teal and wheat
expanse, its slow heave
that from your distance
looks like breathing

and from the birds',
a deeper shade
of fish. The only hook
is a white ship.

Nash ii
after *Landscape in a Dream*

What I always came back to was this:
how the cliffs, flexing in and out of sea,
like a swimmer, and the fudge brown tops,
rolled out the shape of a falcon. And was it
tide pulling in or the land flying out ?

There was sun that made the essential day.
I tried not to look at the other sun, a core
of glistening red like an injury, an exposure,
although it looked at me in the mirror
on the cliff that kept the falcon in view

of himself, and (I thought) unable to fly.
His eye was pitched to the rolling orbs
that began like nested hearts, bindings of twig
or tumble-weed which the mirror ate, calling
them inwards across a burned savannah.

I longed for him to close that view, but he held
open, to the edge of sight, those doors
of shale and spray I stood between.